THE POEM MUST BE SPOKEN

THE POEM MUST BE SPOKEN

Collected Poems 1965-2010

Geoffrey Smith

ISBN: Softcover 978-1-4535-1416-0

This book was printed in the United States of America.

To order additional copies of this book, contact:
Xlibris Corporation
0-800-644-6988
www.xlibrispublishing.co.uk
Orders@Xlibris.co.uk
300492

CONTENTS

Geoffrey Smith's poems have been described as:

Combining wit and tenderness in a very individual and memorable way—they have a delightfully tongue-in-cheek rueful quality about them but a seriousness too which is often profound and moving.

Shelton: Making Steel at Night

Raw power
Fiery splendour
Molten sky

Spreading glow
From Etruria Vale
Shelton steel

A crucible sky
Reddening
The five towns

This is an edited version of my first poem published in Staffordshire Life in 1965

Exploration of a Song Bird Lost in a Fisherman's Hopefulness

Song Bird
        Dancing
On a high tree branch

Song Bird
        Singing
In a night meadow

Fisherman
        Netting
In a pale night sea

Fisherman
        Catching
All the sad sea fish

Orange in
        The sunlight
Silver in the moon

Catch me
        A Song Bird
Fisherman today

This early poem was published by Salisbury Theological College 1967

The Poet in Red Sneakers

Today I bought
A fine pair
Of red sneakers

I thought to myself
If I am going to be a poet again
I'd rather not be
An April showers
Hearts and flowers
Once upon a time
Verses that rhyme
Be my valentine
Kind of poet

No!

I thought to myself
If I'm going to be a poet again
I'd rather be cool
Nobody's fool
Righteously radical
Armed to the teeth
With a real hard edge
In red sneakers
Kind of poet

So!

Today I bought
A fine pair
Of red sneakers

But this was no snap decision
I thought long and hard
I went to the store
And I went back again
I consulted my wife
And I talked with my kids
I studied the sizes
And studied the shades
I tried on the black
And I tried on the grey
I looked at the purple
And considered the green
And thought of a compromise
In orange and blue with pink spots

But at the end of the day
The decision was mine
And I made it
Like men have to do

I just went to the
Store and pointed
Them out and said
Wrap up a pair

Of those highly regarded
Quite world famous boot's
Called 'connors' or 'chuck' or 'converse'
And when asked about colour
I said it quite clear
I'll take red
Make 'em red
Make 'em radically, righteously red

Like the Kremlin at sunset
Or Moscow at dawn
Make them red
Like poetry and blood

Today I bought
A fine pair
Of red sneakers

I'd been up
All the night
With friends who had called
We had drunk
Till the dawn
And talked 'til the bottle was gone

It was that
Kind of night
A fine kind of night
When things become clear
And friendships grow deep and grow strong

And now it was day
And we took things quite slow
As our friends made ready to go
And we rested some more
Until finally I felt it was time

As a mark of this day
And the night we had spent
Of the time that we'd had
And the plans that we laid
And the dreams

So I crossed Harvard Square
With deliberate steps
And bought me a pair
A good, fine, strong pair
Of red sneakers in which to write poems such as this

This poem was written in 1985 and first published at a reading at Harvard University.

Dating the Earliest People in Japan

She would always be up first
Smiling, she would attend to her tasks
Her family were all the same, up before three
They were the earliest people in Japan

And I loved her paper house, the way
Her silk kimono slid to the floor
It never failed to be stimulating
Dating the earliest people in Japan

Her moods were constantly changing
Sometimes at night she'd claim to be tired
Then she'd wake just before three, that's when she'd make me
One of the earliest people in Japan

This poem was joint winner of the Bloodaxe/Evening Chronicle Poetry Competition 1985

The Fine Art of Skimming Stones

My best was
A twelver, twelve
Flat leaps of stones, skimming
Across mill pond water
Like twelve mill stones
Spinning on hot afternoons
Spent, searching for the
Ideal, flat, smooth, rounded
Pebbly stone, comfortable
Between thumb and forefinger
To throw, pulling back with five
Deft fingers, to fly, and spin
Across the water, fascinating children
With my childish skill

Today's Poem, Newcastle Evening Chronicle October 1st 1985

Incident at the Gare du Nord

A final flick / Of the comb
The collar of the black
Leather turned up
The studs burnished
Belt buckled, Levis tight
He heads into the night

The moon filters
Coffee fine through / Cloud cover
He works the stations
Is known to the gendarmerie
Is light on his feet
Moves fast separating
Wallets from pockets
Money from wallets
He quickly discards
Into the waste baskets
On platform nine

Tonight his worst fear
Challenged he runs
Panting, short of breath
The pain in his chest
Echoes against the tunnel's closing
Walls. Out into the night air

Cornered by a young
Gendarme less street wise
Looking for a commendation
In the laser light / And sodium glare
The final flick of the knife
A blade glimmers / A body crumples
Dull on the glistening street

He turns up the collar
Of his leather, studs burnished
And steps into the night
Levis stretched tight
Over the blade he always carries
In the left hip pocket

This poem was a runner up in the Bloodaxe/Evening Chronicle Poetry Competition 1986

Elegy

Her face haunts me now
so much later. Amidst the confusion
of that night her eyes pleaded
Somehow she was the calm at the
centre of the storm, I knew that if
I reached her we would both come
through. Yet, no matter how hard I
struggled, pushing my way through
the crowd, at the end I was no
nearer. As she faded away, I
turned pleading into the light
but couldn't catch the projectionists
eye for detail, when I looked back she was gone
I never did ask her name

Landscapes of the Heart, Canon Books 1986

Resurrection

In this courtyard where grey stone
rises out of nothingness
where earth packs tight
to hold its dead, lest

in time their names forgotten
from memory erased
they fade into insignificance
we cannot bear to face

In the shadow a Cathedral
etched ghostly against moonlight
stands bulwarked strength
against night

And so the dead are named
here in stone
these names from time to time recited
as if known

spelt out, mouthed, names that will
if gently, last
by those who come in search
of past

who find amongst the orchestrated drama
of stone and space
the ordinary dramas of lives recorded

these bones, lying, turned by worm to earth
laid in expectation
of the yearned for possibility
Rebirth

Landscapes of the Heart, Canon Books 1986

Discovering China by Train

They told me this is where you'd be
For all your constant seeking
From Shangai to Peking
Across the China Sea

Following the ancient track
You exchange simple pleasantry
With the local peasantry
Travelling to winter and back

Your peasant shirt is faded
I see you approaching the ferry
At Tunglu wearing your red beret
You look older, perhaps, jaded

The ferry is pursued by a flight of Chinese birds
Seeing you make this transition
Without your usual precision
Such a lack of feeling for words

That's why you feel so much pain
Stumbling around in the wrong sentences
Dropping all your pretences
It's a relief to hear, you're discovering china by train

Written at The Arvon Foundation and Published in Hotlines, Lumb Bank, 1986

To Let: The Perfect Life

forest owners home
own available girl
& beautiful
victorian flatmates
sunbath, corkoplast tiles
library, french polishing
demonstrations &
imaginatively creative dishes

walnut bright
handbound on
unspoilt island

in summary
a perfect life

Written at The Arvon Foundation and Published in Hotlines, Lumb Bank, 1986

Drive-in Love Affair

The night is alive with flying bugs
We catch the soundtrack on channel 97
Watching you on the giant screen I'm in heaven
I'm in love with a goddess in rags

Your long limbed beauty
Shines from the screen beneath the stars
Your silver smile reflects on the cars
When I see you at the drive-in movie

A watery moon climbs into the sky
And we keep our windows closed
As your motives are exposed
The nostalgia makes me high

The windshield fogs over with our breath
I can't see much beyond the hood
Other than your body covered in blood
As the movie ends with your death

I'm in love with an impossible dream
An Ikon of passion, an aching void
A long limbed beauty in celluloid
A star on the drive-in screen

The Poet in Red Sneakers Canon Books 1986

The Swimmers Return

By the poolside swimmers
idle in warm air
moist with breath
and scent of chlorine
behind misted windows

The boys idle time with boasting
as chattering girls pass lazily by along the pool
practising their freestyle in black costumes and bathing caps
that fit skull smooth

I stand at the poolside
considering my dive
into the water below
As people swim by I
recognise a face here and there
I smile, wave back
and then, with a considered gesture
step back from the pools edge

Written after my return from America in 1985

Death in America

As the hot
California sun
burns off mist
the mystery
deepens

The murdered
victim
lies
face down
in the swimming
pool

The prime
Suspect is
interrogated
by a smart
ass cop
and held
for further questioning

bail is set
at a cool $35000

The gardener
saw it all
but he

on account of
his being
deaf
can't tell

So we're left
with only one way:
the true courtroom
drama

Perry Mason
making house calls
takes the case
head on
exposing motive
murderer etc
At the last moment
the prime
suspect
is cut
loose

They lead the
gardener
to the chair
his confession
written
in trembling hand:

I didn't hear the question
can't anyone understand?

I always enjoyed Perry Mason on TV

Silent jiving

Night-time
the band has blown and gone
the lights are up in the dance hall
as the janitor sweeps around
where the couples can still be found
silent jiving

coming and going
dying and thriving
keeping and giving
silent jiving

We go through the motions together
of living our human lives
but the older we get
more broken
the bleaker the vision can seem
so all we can do is keep dancing
silent jiving

Called to a revolution
called to a friends re-union
called to keep hoping and loving
we do the dance we remember
go through the motions by numbers
silent jiving

An exercise in nostalgia

Marriage Guidance

I find this feeling
revealing, love me
she dared, I do he
declared, I love you

Later, she, wearing her
Spare rib apron
'you sink into his arms
to find your arms in his sink'
he called, appalled
by her red hands
and tired eyes

Seeing red, he declared
The washing up waters
divide, your four daughters
dress to kill, take their fill
and leave each night
to delight other parties
Your husbands away
what do you say
shall we see if it's true
that love is like glue

Loving every minute
of it, she giggled
they wriggled, under
the duvet they dived
has your love survived
the fears, years, tears
he enquired? Oh yes
she replied, it's you I always
admired, but it's still
her that I love

I always enjoy the richness of language

Magpies

Magpies scavenge form the past
Steal our futures, fly in pairs
Appear in one's, bring
Poor luck than judgement
'I can't do with magpies'
He said. Unsmiling. Deciding
Something must be done
About the pair nesting in the
Bottom meadow in the elm
By the road. So he took his gun
Down from the shelf
In the kitchen and two
Cartridges, their dull orange
And brass shining caps from the
Box he kept in the
Dresser. I was eager to see
What would be done

I'm left now with nagging
Confused images. Sound
And colour, yellow, green
And the scudding clouds white
Against the summer blue sky

A tantalising glimpse of
Bare flesh, nipple, stomach, thigh
Lovers belly to belly, thrashing
Like beached fish, their gasping
Sound tracking the carnage

Each memory, a ripple
Like silver in the current
Strips of torn foil cascading
From the magpies nest, blown apart
Chicks and all. Silver foil
Crumpled like the reverberating air

Published in New Writing from the North. Midnag 1988

Mrs Thatcher's Fair Isle Knitting Pattern

Knit me a coat
With barbed wire and wool
A coat that will survive
And protect me

A barbed wire wool coat
That won't rust in the rain
A coat that won't stretch twist
Or strain

The old ladies needles
Danced in their hands
As they knitted the coat
She desired

They used plain knit and purl
Cable stitch and stocking
Arran and Fair Isle
and Rib

As with barbed wire
And pain they cast
Stitches in time to complete
Her perfect design

Published in 7 Days (The Communist Party Weekly) January 28th 1989

Good News from Leningrad

Rumours are flooding the town
The price of lemons is dropping fast
Fresh vegetables in the store at last
The consumption of Vodka is down

The news from the west is no fun
Rape, murder, pillage
Threatens every village
The despair affects everyone

Here in Leningrad
The news gets better and better
The interior once dry is now wetter
Things that were worse are just bad

The chairman's lady looking so grand
The heart-throb of the USSR, such style
Her furs and underneath only a smile
Sends a warming glow through the troops in Afghanistan

On T.V. this evening the newscaster was allowed a rare smile
The news was extremely satisfactory
Output is up at the tractor factory
The news just gets better all the while

This poem, also published in 7 Days, attracted a critical letter it was felt not to be PC

A feeling for danger dear Ulrike

Your getaway car
Leaves the police
Fingerprinting
The exhaust clouds
Blue haze

You went through
The library window
Hitting the ground
You slipped through it
Unconventional / As departures go

Since then
You've taken me hostage
Held me in the open
Prison of my fascination
I'm trapped
Like an image on film
Now I feel anxious
Watching the daily news

Captive you captured
My future / I've surrendered
All the possibilities
Now I see you
Bursting through
Concrete walls
Bearing the full
Weight of the law

My recurring nightmare
Getaway cars
Surrounded, flood lit
On a thousand
Anonymous forecourts

I'm constantly
Planning escapes
Making new identities
Expecting to be recognised
At borders

Published in Thursdays Poetry Magazine No 11 June 1988

Memory Songs

The critic says you're
Too consciously writing
POEMS
Let the feelings flow
From the words
Let the emotions run
Riot like kids on the streets
Burning down houses
And looting the shops
Of your mind

Don't worry about form
Or verse or rhyme, the
POEMS
Will come they'll be there
Torn from your subconscious
Stream of consciousness
Like new born children
Fully formed

And when you are in touch
With your feelings
Like this, the
POEMS
Will come

True to the truth
You've discovered

Love songs
From memory's
Juke box

Published in issue 25 of People to People, New writing now in the West Midlands

The Poem must be Spoken

Each day we plan careful progress
Some days are faster
Most are less

But now flowers grow where once there were none
A signature has
Replaced anon

In our garden we plant radish beds
The leaves come first
And then the heads

Each day we attend the newly planted garden
But after rain and sun
The ground begins to harden

But still the miracle is renewed
A delicate tracery
Of roots and stalks force through

The ground is hard and must be broken
As the poem, to be heard
Must first be spoken

This poem appeared first in Thursdays and later the magazine Christian, issue14 1989

A Fragment

Footsteps outside the
Window, the tread of
Feet on gravel, the
Visitors who pause

And go their way
Their unanswered knock
Echoing in the empty hall
Way of our hearts. Left alone

We measure distance
Casting the stone
Into the hearts well
And counting the moments

Until the distant echo tells
How far we are apart
How lonely passions
Separate us. This continuing
Drama of our love

Published in Landscapes of the Heart, Canon Books, Newcastle and Christian 1988 and collected in New Christian Poetry Ed Alwyn Marriage 1990

Visiting Josephine Butler's Grave at Kirknewton Churchyard

Screech of peacock
Across a still day

On the road verge
Peacock feathers
Tasselled ribs
Collected
For a brighter memento

Celandine in the stream

Birdsong bee drone

Lichen on the gravestone

Fingers tracing
Time-blurred letters
In warm stone
Such strong passion
Drowned in grief
And transformed

Collected in New Christian Poetry Ed Alwyn Marriage 1990

Prayer Walk

Pausing at each station
to reflect on the goodness of God
and the glory of created things

We offer hymns in unison
with the birdsong and bee drone
our voices stilling the beating
of butterflys wings
startling the sheep
who look up
from solemn grazing

A high Sun filters
through trees
shadowing the ground
with clerestory light

We enter the vast crossing
beneath the mountain
where a congregation of herdwick
greets the procession
with startled eyes
as it emerges
from the darkened nave
and the celebration begins

Bread made of earth
ground between mountains

Wine spilling
from deeper springs

Published in Christian: Summer 1995

In the Chapel at Dornie, Wester Ross

The place is set for a small Eucharist
In the chapel still smelling of newness
Under its roof of compressed straw
A congregation is gathered
Visitors from Glasgow and the south

To start the service, ritual prescribes
The choosing of the hymns
The preparation of the altar, adorning
Oneself in Eucharistic vestments
The lighting of the candles, which is why
In the stillness of the cloud riven
Morning, eyes fixed on the back of my neck
I struggle to strike the damp, highland
Matches on the soft box
Before the word can be spoken or the bread broken

Collected in A Touch of Flame Ed Jenny Robertson 1989

A Poem on your Birthday

This is the day to rise to the occasion
In time, in experience, with elation
The turning of the year, your anniversary
Demands from me a special bursary
A gift that bequests its own kind of pleasure
The memory of which in days to come you will treasure

Your life has been marked with loss and pain
Your parents dying when you were least able to explain
The meaning of loss and the loneliness growing
As you raised your own children knowing
How much pleasure they would have given your
Parents who they in return would have adored

The loss of your health to a chronic illness
The increased dependency costing you more not less
The times and days through which you have passed
Living each to the full, as the days dance past
It would be good if our new life together
Could enjoy a brief spell of more settled weather

You have grown older, wiser, more mature
My aim today is to do my utmost to ensure
That the days which lie ahead are filled
So that seductive siren voices can be stilled
That constantly argue, there should be more
We're missing out; there is now only a memory store

From today we can recommit our friendship
Drink a satisfying draft from the loving cup
Take each day as it comes as though it were a gift
Designed to take our spirits and lift
Them so that we can walk through these autumn days
Of our life with a spring in our step as we find new ways

Written for my wife Janet to celebrate her birthday in 2007

A Translation from the Portugese

Poetry is all artifice and tricks
Making new art from old licks
Poets inventing pain they are not feeling
From the work of others, unaware they must be stealing

Sometimes they read the writing
And transfer as they are reading
Emotions, stresses, heartaches and strain
You cannot fairly steal another's pain

So round they go these written verses
Each adapting to renewed purpose
Quite leaving reader and writer out of breath
Like a stunt rider on the wall of death

Published in Lyrics of Life, United Press

Imagine this

Imagine this
A picture painted with words
A distant landscape
Figures pressing forward
A progress, crowds
Obscuring the central
Character, dust, a hazy sun

Imagine drawing
Closer, hearing
Sound carried on still air
A cry of pain, an angry shout
The sound of leather tearing flesh
A wounded animal scream

Imagine drawing nearer still
Imagine the smell
Of sweat stained bodies
Mingled scents, the smell of raw wounds
The cloying sweetness of blood

Imagine blinking
Missing the final scene
The body lifted
High, the puzzled
Onlookers uncertainty
At what is taking place,
Drifting away

Imagine, from a safe
Distance, looking
Back at the scene
Three figures on three trees
And at the foot of the middle tree
Two kneeling, a man
A woman weeping and a voice

If you sing, sing my name
let your words echo my virtue not my shame

A reflection on vocation

Radio Therapy

Your endurance
is legendary, arms
outstretched as if
to embrace this
healing ray or ray of death
whatever the hell it is
only time will tell
How you as a target
of their concern
bear your breasts
patiently in dignified
suffering

A crucified Madonna
dying a little each day
giving life
to those you love

Written whilst watching my wife Janet's radio therapy treatment for breast cancer

Slow Lane

It's all the rage now
taking it slow
easing into the day
my former up and at 'em
style is passé now

Now I dance
to the slow rhythm
of the weeks pulse
where entropy
pervades.

The diary I have never
kept counts back
from Friday one day
at a time

Until Monday
passes and is gone
forever.

Painful adjustments can make you the envy of others and sorry for yourself

Shere Gullion

Shere Gullion is clothed
In mist and myth
Words whispered by
The whipping wind

Sure it takes the words
Right off yer mouth

Here in this brackish
Water, Fin McCool
Was bewitched
By the weeping maiden

Sure she was so pretty
She was, she was

History and mystery
Unfolds with the tears
And years of troubles
Fought and lost
On this bracken slope

Sure the giants play
A thunderous game today

The hillside is littered
With burnt out cars
Where Joe Cool practises
Handbrake turns, re-writes
The myths of troubled times
And the maiden still weeps

Sure he's one of them all right
Keep yer fecking mouth shut, OK

The RUC secure
Behind galvanised steel
The tri-colour dances
On the uneasy wind

Found as a note written after a sponsored walk in South Armargh

Air Raid

Black hawk hovering
On wings of mouse
A silent presence
Punctuating the grey
Pages of the sky

Beneath the animals
Fear prickling fur
As the scurry
Sheltering under the russet
Rustling autumn leaves

Small hearts fast
Pulsing till the lark
Rises to sound
The all clear

A poem written at a writing workshop in Northumberland

From our Yachting Correspondent

(A translation from the Dutch)

Day 14 of our passage
Still the unfamiliar sea
Stretches to the anonymous
Horizon, taunting

The wind from the south
Fills the sail fitfully
With idle gusts
We drift with the currents
Like sea kelp, flotsam
Of squandered lives

We speak of tying up for the night
Against an unfamiliar
Quayside. Long to be awakened
By strange accents
And a new language

Not a translation. nor is it about yachting

Awakening

It was another of those moments
like fine wine turned to vinegar
and decanted. There was
only silence left in the glass
lying on the bedroom floor

a spillage from
its gaping mouth, like a wound
seeping into the carpet.

It was the only clue
that you had been here
the silence and a chiffon
scarf draped idly
over the end of the bed

an early morning sun
seeped through the half closed curtains
picking out the note
lying in the dust on the dresser

This was a poetry competition winner at Fircroft College, Birmingham

The Water Meadows Salisbury—1967

days are drawn out as we move into a future of untested promise
as in a meadow scented with new mown grass

in these meadows a thousand years were celebrated
and in those Sweet Vernal days I celebrated meeting you

for Fisher, Constable pictures the graceful beauty of the spire
as I now picture your graceful beauty and your Lady's Smock

An exercise based on the word 'Meadow' for my writing workshop

Creed River

Turbulence of peat
Brown water, Salmon
Sing their spawning song

Tuned to the rivers
Symphony the chorus
Rises like psalms

Gaelic echoes, language
As old as these hills
As the spawning memory

Of these gallant
Majestic fish, lissom
Silver in the peat brown water

In truth there were more poems than fish

The Church of the Sunday Jazz

The church of the Sunday jazz
Gathers on the first Sunday
Of each month
To worship
At the altar of funk

Whether in heaven with Stephan
Or playing classics with Stan
The time signatures
With a modernist twist
Worship at the altar of funk

The church of the Sunday jazz
Gathers on the first Sunday
Bringing the cool to the borders
New York sophistication
To worship at the altar of funk

Playing the blues, paying their dues
Players keep their rhythms strict
As they divide time between sets
Honouring the heroes of jazz
At the altar of funk

I wrote this to celebrate the Sunday Jazz concerts at The Buccleuch Centre in Langholm it was published on the Mungrizedale writers web-site and was the title poem of The Church of the Sunday Jazz chap book

I Come into the Presence of Still Water

Resting in quiet pools
As giddy waters roar past

Floating in a gentle eddy
In this quiet backwater

Where dappled trout rest under trees
camouflaged by a dappling sun

As with Larkin's invented religion
Dedicated and named from water

I come into the presence
Of still water, to find faith

In the gentle support of the stream
I rest in the dream of peace and more

Water bears my weightless self
dappled trout nibble my toes

An exercise written for my first Mungrisedale writers meeting

The Night Shift Chocolate Awards

The lights in the chocolate factory windows
Are switched off one by one
Production of dark chocolate gives way to milk

Each desperate demand for assistance
Is greeted with scorn by our competitors
The governing and the governed enjoy our chocolate bars

Cautiously feeling your way to coincidence
You shed skins revealing
The pulsating beauty of milk white flesh

After reviewing his fleet with measured tread
And one hand inside his vest
The Red Admiral defects
For new found prosperity in the west

After destroying your instructions you meet him at dawn
On a shingle shore, signaling with a shuttered lamp
As his submarine noses its way onto land
You wish you had bothered to dress
Offering his hand he whispers is it true that
There's a glass and a half in each breast?

Knowing that a broad alliance of money and culture
Threatens the destruction of all you hold dear
You suckle the child at your breast

Like a giant his eyes open wide
His small hand paws at your blue veined skin
Settling his head he falls asleep, just then
The lights in the chocolate factory announce
Another run of dark chocolate has begun

An exercise in surrealism published in People to People Issue 9

The Natural Theology of Rivers

The story unfolds
In stages as the cloud
Lifts and gathers the snowy sagas
On the high peaks.
We drive through these torturous
Narrow roads, climbing
To the watershed

Storm driven under
Dour skies, grey curtains
Of raw weather wash
The ice white of the glaciers
Blue waters, trapping the memories
Of a thousand summer skies

Streams cascade through
Forested slopes, long plumed
Fingers reaching down, wrapping
The mountains like wires
Gathering force into icy
Depths, stirring the deep
Fathomed water, boiling
The surface white

This gathering power
Of water forces itself
Through a narrow gateway
Of hard stone, haunches
Lifted, twisted, forced,
Through the narrowing gap
Granting power to
the raging river

The animus of this natural
Force conjures from those
Along its way the image
Of another deeper life
Beyond their own imagining
Spirits of nature, dancing
Dancing, weaving, inter-weaving
Stories of threat and promise

This force demands respect
Requires sacrifice
As it passes under the seven
Stone arches of the low
Bridge washing the bones
Of the sacrificed

Satiated waters force subdued
Energy tamed, gentled by the contours
In the valley floor as the river weaves
And wanders slowly streaming through
A rich landscape to mingle fresh waters with salt.

Written in Norway in 2008

The Arithmetic of Love

The maquette sits on the dust
specked window sill
these unheeding lovers enjoy
endless tantric sex
a permanent state of nirvana
orgasm, bliss, sun kissed ceramic skin

For forty years it has been placed
in house after house, but only for the last
twenty, have we been safe from its spell

In the beginning, rows would flare without warning
cross words, criticism, anger, pain
and later as we tenderly kissed
our bruised bodies and our egos
we might notice that a jarring
sudden movement or gentle breeze
had caused our tantric lovers to fall apart
her open loins revealed, his erection exposed, raw

Over the years we did the arithmetic
of love, two and two became four
and after one particular, painful exchange
when divorce seemed all but inevitable
we agreed that the power of the maquette
should be contained at last

It sits, as it has for twenty
years now, on dust speckled window sills
unheeding lovers in their close
embrace, bathed now in soft Cumbrian light

We look and smile and wonder
at this symbol of settled state
and trust the Blue-Tack will hold
our lovers in their contained passion

A mystery yet to be explained

Symmetries

Of life's symmetries
There is, it seems no ending
As truth follows falsehood or day
Night these juxtapositions
Of grace, which some chose to call God
Some choose to call by other names
Whilst not denying the symmetry

As when in the deep loss of love
When grief numbs the soul
So often, it seems, the promise
Of new life can seem as the dawn
Rising on a still morning promising
So much that is new whilst remaining
In essence the very same

Death often requires patient
Waiting, as the dying prepare to leave
The shell of this life as a kernel
Sheds the husk until the final rattle
Signifies the end of life

Just as in its own way
Birth too requires waiting, less patient
Perhaps as the newly born
Finally determines that its time has come
And bursts into the present
Drawing a first hungry breath, announcing
It's joy at this new thing

Of life's symmetry
There is it seems no ending
As re-birth, resurrection
Follows death and its silence
This juxtaposition of grace
Some choose to call God
Or simply see coincidence
Whilst recognizing the symmetry

A poem written in response to a 'phone call from a friend to tell me that he was to become a grandfather

The Dangers of Fire

beat the body down crushed bones into flames
the roaring fires all consuming energy sparked
to the stake he comes embraces naked flames
beat the body down crushed bones boiling blood
the rich mix calcium phosphate glowing
with his right hand embraces wood and fire
bright holograms pictures a face his beard on fire
sightless now incandescent candescent acrid stench
no beauty here just the beaten body burning
the fire gets up he neither stirs or cries
unrepentant unprotesting shriven annealed
friend of king but not of queens or rome
they beat the body down into crushed bones of ash damp earth
words remain the book remains they cannot burn the book
the psalms are recited vulgar words remain even as
they beat the body down as fire draws his life out
with indrawn fiery breath he draws back his words
they beat the body down scatter crushed bones to the wind
unsudden death comes slow lightning sparks tempestuous fire
this pain more than I can bear I am beaten into earthen ends

A meditation on the death of Thomas Cranmer

The Rain (after Hernandez)

Still fields, A feeling of rain
The cattle lying, low cloud
on the fell. The gravedigger
cuts a trench in cemetery earth

Uncovering the earlier dead,
flattening the bones
into trenched earth
beneath a weeping sky

During the night the trench
will fill with water, in the morning
it will be pumped dry, leaving
a fragrance of damp earth

The cortege approaches steady
as the falling rain, footsteps
shuffling on a damp path
splashing through puddles

The silence concentrates
as the coffin is laid to rest
The dead know peace, rain chills
the mourners huddle together
concentrate to hear the words recited
over the dead, who lie soundless in their wooden vestments

Around the graveyard the trees
lean in to the gathering darkness
as if listening to the words, their roots
curling through earth. Under the shadow
of the guardian trees
the passion of water deepens

I wrote this after reading Hernandez the Spanish civil war poet in translation

Invasion

I sit up in a strange bed
Krupa playing a drum solo in my head

Wondering who you were and whether
I had ever asked your name

before we slipped between the sheets
making love into the oblivion of early morning

Too much wine, slipping like velvet
down my dry throat, more wine is always less

Too much is never enough, nodding
to our hostess, who brings another bottle

I sit up in a strange bed, look at
your sleeping form and give thanks

I've occupied a whole country
without benefit of either armour or tanks

A morning after the night before poem

Dragonflies over Basra

Across the water, iridescence
in bright summer air
reflects rainbow light
As pulsing wings shimmer
Above the desert town

The hollow emptiness of the day
against blue sky, shadows
shape and form, muezzins' calls
drift across the water

A harsh pulsing of rotors
Warm air winnowing
the nights' noisescape
the bitter bite of bullets
the dragonflies night assault

This poem was written at the time of the war in Iraq

St Seburg, August 19th

Nuremburg notes
Wagnerian voluntaries
soar across history's broad reaches

This damp August
day we recall St Seburg
remembered for his miracles
transforming frozen waste to fire

Icicles' sharp crackle
Diamante lights sparkle
their encased brilliance
released, teasing the eye
with shards of icicle fire

Seburg, Nuremburg
trial by fire, the world's thirst for justice
Seburgs' constant prayer

Another war themed poem written on St Seburg's day

Squantum

Explorations in literature, hardbacks
crunch underfoot, soft backs
give gently beneath our toes
Words shattered, sentences deconstructed
paragraphs parsed, essays précised
to within a column inch of their lives

Literature junkies hang out partying
in the stacks, stumbling around in the wrong sentences
such a lack of feeling for words
The literary jungle is home to a rebel army
past participles reclassified, nouns lost
in the enjambments of time

Manifesto's loaded with conjugated
verbs, magazines full of rhetoric, speeches
recorded as inspiration for future generations

Occasionally I like to write about the art of writing

Speed Dating @ 60

1959, 100 mph on a 57 Vincent
Me, thrilled to be alive, two up
on the Preston by-pass. Since then
I've loved to travel fast speed dating at 60,
watching the road disappear beneath my tyres
on the edge of control, the wind
whipping breath and words away

Accelerating past 60, poems lost
in the slipstream as the motorcycle I ride
becomes an iron horse in the gasoline age
Now I want to make a date with destiny
just me alone, on my bike
accelerating into the unknown, my epitaph
No more dating at 60, he's gone on his final ride.

Published as part of a Mungrisedale writers anthology Dating at 60 Valentines day 2009

Anticipation

A low sun etching
The grey sky with gold
Waking next to you
The two of us once so fetching
Now growing disgracefully old

Dreaming like the movies
Naked like film stars
Planning the future true
Here we are old lovers
Hanging round the bars

Maintaining our habits together
Getting high on our hopes
Climbing for a better view
Observing the changing weather
Bouncing off the ropes

Consciously changing direction
Keeping the pace real slow
Me relying on you
Negotiating a life extension
Reaping what we sow

Published in Christian May/June 1989

Travelling Companions

I see your reflection
In the windows of the train

Your half smiling reverie
Your half expressed disdain

My covert glance
Avoids your eyes

Admiring the view
I invent seductive lies

Of course you notice my gauche look
Whilst pretending to read your book

The train rattles south
Clattering through idle rural halts

The stops that we make unscheduled
By points or crossing faults

From time to time
You cross and uncross your legs

The electrifying kiss of sheer nylon
You can't make omelettes without breaking eggs

Sends shock waves tingling in my spine
In the reflection I catch your smiling sign

Published in Rhymes of Passion in 1990

I'm

I'm here and waiting in vain
I'm sixty and dating again
I'm uncertain about what to do next
I'm not used to dating by text
I'm loving this modern age
I'm clear that www is all the rage
I'm thinking of offering you dinner
I'm thinking we might become sinners
I'm keen to make you my lover
I'm thinking only of you and no other
I'm tired of sending my own valentines
I'm hoping for one that says will you be mine

Written as a contribution to dating at 60, Mungrisedale Writers 2009

Sonnet of the deceitful speed dater

First, the Japanese creative writer
We smile and run out of conversation
Next the Polish lady, a nail biter,
was too tense beneath her false elation
So on we moved to another table
My third was French, a young mademoiselle
She left just as soon as she was able
I watch her waiting for the all change bell
And on we move again, this common round

Then I see your face and hear your bitter words
When I 'phoned to say I wouldn't be round
I thought University of the Third
Age, was an excellent cover for me
Yours was the last face I thought I would see

Published as part of a Mungrisedale writers anthology Dating at 60 Valentines day 2009

Requiem

The surreal quality of the light
the air, the sounds of the night
echo in the square

The complex history of shadows
the interplay of earth and blood
the winter sun

the promenade fills the busy
streets with crowds

In our attics high above, pigeons bring
messages with greetings
from those we love

Written during a writing holiday in Barcelona 2008

Skye Scape

Intermittent pulses of soft
Rain, interspersed with sun

A strong breeze blowing
Constantly from the outer Isles

The arched proscenium
Of the rainbow the colour of tweed

The seascape a constant filtering of light
Adjusting for colour and reception

Horizontal and vertical holds
Failing as sun makes way for rain

On the sea at low water, tide wrack
The water fitful, anxious to return

Watching the tide on Skye whilst waiting for the ferry

Dr Johnson's Request

Each word bore the weight of meaning
Was given definition tending to plain speaking

At the end, Dr Johnson enquired of his executor
Where do you intend to bury me?

'In the Abbey', replied Sir John, 'where else
Do you expect to be laid to rest?'

'If that is to be the case' the Doctor replied
'Then lay a stone to protect my body'

Knowing that his physical body
Would perish whilst the body of his work
Required no such protection

Dr Johnson edited the first English Language Dictionary

The Poem will be Slow

Preparing myself in order
to be ready to fly
I think the poem will be slow
exhaled like a sigh
As we look down on the border
you reach out to the shadow on the land
tracing its movement on the window
with your soft and gentle hand
questioning the disorder
that has come into your day
you watch the world turning below
and then turn slowly away

Written in 1985 on a flight to the USA with my wife and young family

In the Horn of the Moon Cafe

In the Horn of the Moon Café
by the iron bridge
we took our leave over lunch
broke bread together, spilled the wine

I remember it rained
as we turned onto 89
travelling south
to the airport

Already the memories fade
surely there was more
to it than photographs
in a drawer

And no matter
where I look I cannot find
the photo I took
of the Horn in the Moon Cafe

Written after a lunch with friends in Vermont before flying back to England

Sculpture

Beneath the terrain
Of the Hebrides
The earth shifts
And settles

Polished earth
Polished stone
Hills and valleys
In settled corrugation
And contour

In these hills
And sea scoured lochs
The images of mirrored stone
Concave and convex
Reflect the human
Artifice the shapes
And shadows

We pause to view
A sculpture
Its drama contained
In the poise of the stone
The tension that holds
It in place in the landscape

But the guidebook
Has no record of the artist
Or of its making
Or placing, this is a natural
Stone placed by glacial energy
Or tectonic force
To be respected
Ploughed around
And left to stand
Over times stillness

Written on the Isle of Lewis

Salmon Rise

When the salmon run
time is lost
peat dark pools
appear in my eyes

When the salmon run
Sea falls below
the equinox and my heart
sings a new song

The lamps are set
for an early rise
Thermos coffee
by the waters edge

When the salmon run
rippling the waters surface
silver flashes
in the rivers song

The fishing on Lewis was excellent if I had been more skilled as a fishermen

Chocolate Words

If poetry was chocolate
I would offer you
mouth to mouth
recitation

Published in The Church of the Sunday Jazz 2009

Cody to Dieppe

From Marlow to York
There is talk
But never a crossword
In jest or otherwise I heard

From the barrier reef
To Nazca or Cuzco in Peru
I will follow you
To the ends of the earth
Your scent is become my passion

I long to become accustomed
To your presence
If only the depth can be plumbed
Join me for a journey just a short hop
As we set sail on Cody to Dieppe

Published in The Church of the Sunday Jazz 2009

The Retreat

'. . . . . you are here to kneel, where prayer has been valid. And prayer is more than an order of words, the conscious occupation of the praying mind, or the sound of the voice praying' TS Eliot Little Gidding

The House Martins
Are building again
Their nests of mud
Thatched into the under eaves
Of the house

This constant attention
To the detail of the task
Finds echoes
In the birdsong, bee drone
Of this English summer day

Natures tapestry
Weaves its pattern, Eliot's
Voluptuary sweetness
Erupts around us in profusions
Luxuriant green intoxicating scents

Deep rose embers
Of the fire which once
burned in the bud

And we are here for prayer
To dip into the deep
Flowing stream of prayer which
Across time has acquired its own validity

The precious sentimentality
Of the scraps of memory
Thought and unfulfilled aspiration
Are pieced together
In a patchwork design

We throw over our bed as we sleep
Embraced in warmth
Our dreams help us make sense
Of what was, what is, what is yet to be

Published in The Church of the Sunday Jazz 2009

The Drowning Man Serenaded by Bells

The drowning man
Face down in the mill race
Was drawn by the sluice
At an accelerating pace

The river powerfully roars
The mill wheels slowly grind
And as he drifts past
No one seems to mind

They couldn't hear his gurgles
As he floats past singing
There is the comforting sound
Of church bells ringing

Published in The Church of the Sunday Jazz 2009

Ward Ten

Unsung heroes
Of Forty-Seven
Waiting anxiously
At the front

Called to arms
By volunteers
From the Fifth
Awaiting the whistle

Going over the top
Charging the advance
Paying the price
Wounded in the wardroom

Exchanging signals
Becoming clear
About ends and means
Resisting a fresh attack

Unsung heroes
Of Forty-Seven
Gathered for a re-union
In Ward Ten

They tell tall tales
About the wounds
They won in the attack
Resisting the charge

Now it's almost too late
To tell how the battle will end
The registrar's round
Finally settles the matter

Written following a brief stay in hospital

The Fulmar

The Fulmar feeds and flies. In the gales' bitter teeth.
Strong winds chill the bones. This land of saints and tides.
In the Island church prayers for the dead and dying.
Memory imprinted in the genetic blueprint of a people.
Not the Saints imprint but the unsanctified.
Across hostile waters that will win in the end.
Swamp these lands and wash out the memory
Unsettle the settlements and turn the village to raw
Earth, sand dunes. Scatter the sheep. Unfold the lambs.
Listen carefully to the caterwauling wind
This thin place between heaven and earth
This place of quiet death. Of wailing birth

Regional winner, National Poetry anthology 2009 and published in The Church of the Sunday Jazz 2009

A Silence of Bees

Occasionally you draw attention to the silence in the garden
This long summer, that arrived full of barbeque promise
And ended with the constancy of rain falling steadily, between
The breakfast tea and honey toast and the evening G&T

Occasionally the silence echoes, despite the breeze stirring the willow, What
is missing? The golden drone of the bee raiding the lavender
Spreading the heavy scent of roses after interminable summer showers
Nosing here and there into the flower heads, drawing out the sweetness

Occasionally we share our concern, draw each others attention
To the silence before reacting with pleasure when we see and hear
The approaching drone of the by now, infrequent, summer visitor
Whose appearance is of hushed wings drumming the air after rain

Occasionally the single visitor, welcomes and disturbs, a stark reminder
Of human neglect, environmental hostilities arrayed against the bee
Our missing summer visitor whose absence is noted by the stillness
We hear and whose message we ignore between the dismal headlines

Occasionally we stop to imagine the worst should the pollination end
Imagine the dreadful impossibility, surely there couldn't be, a Wimbledon
Without Strawberries, a world without apples or softer fruits or Cattle
Feed, a barren silent spring world of abandoned crops left to fail

Occasionally we are reminded, the bee works hard at this task
Pollination is the miracle that sustains our lives, working to nurture
The Queen, so we, at the end of the day in our flower rich, colour rich,
scented garden's riotous display, can raise our glass, to toast the bee

Mungrisedale Writers website

Compline

Devil's Bit Scabious, Knapweed, Meadowsweet, Wild Angelica
Twenty four hours in the natural history of the fell, time lapsed
Sphagnum Moss and Bog Rosemary decorate the landscape
Still the shadows play on the oils, dawn turns to dusk, night falls
Sun rises, an abstraction holding and revealing night fears

In the safety of each others arms, as darkness falls, we watch the sun
Setting on an indigo fell, each morning the same sun teases us
Into wakefulness as dawn rises over curlew and grouse

The painting, too large for any other space, finds new purpose here
We recall the video camera tracking the fells life from dawn to dawning
We know the solace of welcoming night and rising to new challenges
Where the deep abstraction of the paintings' blocks of hued oils
Capture the warmth of day, the chill of night, rumours of love

Each night we embrace St Francis' '*little death',* surrender ourselves
To the days dying, whilst in the stream outside the open window
The otter follows rumours of eel under the fells long shadow

On each bedside table a picture of mothers, yours and mine
Like sainted angels at prayer they keep watch, present and absent
Still softly singing, thro' the livelong night, familiar words that comfort
Matthew, Mark, Luke and John, Bless the bed that they lie on

Mungrisedale Writers workshop

Conchita Cintron: Rejoneadora

Conchita! the cry, echoes from the walls
Conchita! the crowds acclaim
Conchita! their darling, rides
In the parade of the Matadors
Through cheering crowds along Plaza de Linares,

On her last fight in Spain she rides, Rejoneadora
As tradition requires, then turns
For permission to the box of the Presidente
Denied, she dismounts to confront the bull as Matadora

Sword and cape raised the bull charges
She lowers her sword to the sand, Feigning
The final blow, with her fingers she offers a gentle feminine caress
Between the massive, muscled shoulders

So different from those first abbatoir kills
When she practiced her skills, in a Tango with the doomed bulls
Who danced to their bragging song until with opened eyes
She learned the tender spot behind the horns

On this one day in Franco's Spain
The svelte Rejoneadora confronts tradition and history
A feminine icon drawn in the blood and sand of the bullring
With calm composure facing twelve hundred
Pounds of enraged bull, she seduced the crowds

Conchita! the cry echoes from the walls
Conchita! the audience roars
Brag sweet tenor bull
Conchita! The Sweet Matadora;
Leaves the arena crushing blood red
Carnations with each soft tread

Entered into the Basil Bunting Award 2009

Over Breakfast Conversation is No Longer Necessary

The spoon stirs the soft flakes
Of oat into the bowl, reflectively
I read the news, of snowflakes
Settling on the towns around
Leaving only the absence of sound

At the table I pour the tea
Into the days first cup and think
Ahead to what that lies before me
As in the stillness of this gentle start
I hear the soft ticking of times heart

The library clock above the bookshelves
Whispers the minutes one by one
Lost in the crossword I count the clues
And imagine I hear your tongue as you sip
Lick soft crumbs from your upper lip

These quiet days time passes slow
No hurrying to beat the rush hour
No fierce winding of the engine
To start the car and roar noisily away
Now I settle slowly to enjoy the day

Entered into the Mirehouse Competition 2009

Kindness

The ease with which
We spend our time
Together in the company
Of those we call our friends
Is shaped by the learning
At our mothers breast
Where we discover
The best of each other
And ourselves
So kindness
Becomes the currency
Through which our lives
Are expanded
And human virtue
And it's many values
Defended

A 'found' poem pencilled in my handwriting on the fly leaf of a book I was reading

Building a Cathedral as a Defence Against Entropy

All around the sound
Of falling light
Soon it will enclose
The trees and animals
Of the wilderness there

And then when darkness
Has enclosed everything
And nothing disturbs
The stillness that lies
Far beyond sound

Then the gods will be sensed
As dwelling amongst us
Discerning the truth
Of the worlds anguish
And human defiance

And over time the dark
Will be pierced by starlight
The moon ringed by refracted light
And a cathedral
Built in the forest canopy
To defend us from what lies
Beyond knowing

A poem on the theme of silence

Cineri Gloria Sera Venit

We walk, a hundred hundred men, the ground trembles
Under sandaled feet, a rich mix this legion
Drawn from the furthest reaches of empire
We make good time along this melancholy shore
Damp salt encrusted marsh plants crushed beneath
Marching feet following the road east into the distance
An empire over which the sun never sets warming our backs
Dazzling us as it glances off the ocean crimson

Today as we walk the shoreline there is litter
Along the way stones return to sand lapped by gentle tides
Here and there chisel marks on the bricks, ruined houses, walls
Buildings, shelters along the way, life's detritus
Plastic, glass, thrown maybe from the ferries
Plowing their steady furrow across the ocean
Their daily ritual coming, going, arriving, departing
Mournful echoes, fog horns on the night air

This is the life journey we make, steady progress
Into a final dark distantly lit by the lights
Of an unknown city. A city of promise or hope
We choose to enter its walls, passing through its gates
Journey's end, uncertainty, a laurel wreath, a crown
Silent praise of angel's song

This solitary life is an act of faith. It is hard to keep
Loving, walking, just one uncertain step in front of another
Step, 'cineri gloria sera venit' fame to the dead comes too late

This poem was placed third place in the Senhouse Competition 2009

Approaching the Latin Primer

Accents, ancient voices, dialects and language
Chatter on the airwaves
Common voices consistent across history
Common wealth, common parlance
Voices in unison, songs in Solway air
Under marching feet the ground trembles
Remember *deficit omne quod nasciture*
Everything that is born passes away
Legions draw near imposing the common
Legislature of governance, *Pax*
Romana, the language reflects
Authority imposed across a world
Slowly becoming revealed
fortiter in re, suaviter in modo
Resolute in action, gentle in manner.
A single expression of unity, purpose and intention

Entered into the Senhouse Competition 2009

De Mortuis Nil Nisi Bonum
Of the Dead [Say] Nothing but Good (Horace)

Their fingers trace a small depression in damp sand
A slender ridge snakes around the depression
Their excavation reveals first the back
And after gentle probing, the tail and head
Wild boar the twentieth legion has been here
Fought and fallen, victorious and defeated

This powerful dangerous predatory animal lies
One cheek pressed to damp sand
As tides rise and fall, the figure is now covered
Now revealed, half covered or half revealed
The salt lick corrodes the soft sand stone
At low water as sun rises, the glow
From the east bathes the stone in clear chill light

But now at high water as sun sets
A warm red sun reflects in stone eyes
A flashing wild embattled symbol of the virtues

Entered into the Senhouse Competition 2009

Parker 51

I have looked everywhere, searched, oh for years, but somehow
Somewhere, my vintage, maroon, Parker 51 fountain pen, has gone
It was a gift for an aspiring writer to fill the page, a coming of age
Present from my mother, dead now for thirty years, though tears
Still flow when I think of her my moral centre in changing times, signs
Of change, my own children with children of their own, are grown

Then recently on e-bay, idly surfing I found the very thing, inspiring
Me to bid on a Parker 51in the original presentation, I won the auction
A seasoned e-buyer, within days I was holding again, the maroon pen
I first used forty three years ago, to write a thank you note, I quote
Dear mum, I am writing this letter, my handwriting has just got better
But to the e-bay seller a formal e-mail from her buyer, to say hi'ya
I have turned the house upside down for years, there have been tears
Of frustration, so thanks, I can now write the words I have seen and heard

Entered into the Mirehouse Competition 2008

The Peacocks Tears

In the bomb makers workshop on the dusty floor
Of an anonymous bungalow In Kabul
Bleach and fertilizer mix with dung and the dust

Here at night the peacocks roost in the high branches
By the edge of a moonlight bright stream

Pipes roughly sawn to size, spill steel filings to the floor
Detritus fizzing with spilt bleach
Coils of fishing wire and Flowers of Sulphur

Peahens gather beneath the trees in the waning moon
They conceive in the moments before a rising sun

The prize for this handiwork, a place amongst the martyrs of faith
Time spent with the virgins waiting in paradise, but first
The treacherous bombs have to be planted

Peacocks' tears glisten beneath his eyes
As the pea hen sips tears from his cheeks

They wait for the approaching
Patrol, the young soldiers' naïve, intent on survival
Queen and Country, treading cautiously

The only sound the pullulating of the eggs and, later still
The young birds tap, tapping on the hard shell

A boot snags the fishing line, triggered
The bomb blast dazzles and blinds
Scorching the dry Afghan earth

A Peacocks cry echoes across the cracked air.

Entered into the Basil Bunting Award 2009

Incoming Tide: Maryport

Rising tide
Spills onto
Darkening
Sand

Filling rock
Pools with
The heady
Brew

A viscous
Mix of salt
Water and sand
Black like
Guinness
Filling a glass

As the pools
Fill, foam spreads
Across their surface
Like brewers yeast
In the first mash

Written whilst watching the tide rise

Re-reading the Greeks in Mexico

Ornate coffins in a shop window, death on display. Louring over the town, the Volcano, ground trembling. By the bus station, the bus to Mexico City ready to leave. In the darkness the bus headlights illuminating the torn year old poster of de Souza whose election a year ago had started the troubles, that and the anxious crowd waiting for the eruption. The child's poster in the church showing the angry figure of God pointing, the volcano spewing red hot larva, they said the dust settled on Mexico City as the giant plumb line in the Cathedral swung gently to and fro. The bus roared down the freeway towards Mexico City an hour away, suddenly the driver swore, in the headlights a pack of wild dogs in the road, and then the banging of the dogs underneath the bus, death on the highway, he turned in the wake of the bus, lying on the tarmac, the corpses of maybe three, maybe four, dogs, eviscerated, bleeding, too dead to whimper.

The bus pulled into Puebla. He got off. The café was dark, despite the morning sun. She sat in the shadows waiting quietly. He ordered ham and eggs and coffee. They looked at each other in silence. His eggs arrived, he ate in silence. She slowly, carefully, smoked a cigarette and then stubbed the end into her coffee cup. She called to the waiter, café solo, he started to pour the jug into her cup then saw the cigarette end, sighed and turned to take a new cup which he carefully filled and handed to her.

So how is the poetry she asked? He smiled, its fine I'm re-reading the Greeks, you know how it is with the Greeks, best to start with Homer. As Lao Tzu says the longest journey starts with the first step. Then there will be Aeschylus, Sophocles, Euripides, Plato, they all have their have their place in the scheme of things. And death? She asked, how will you deal with death? Metepec is always the best for coffins, he replied cautiously, ornate, adorned, lacquered coffins that can be born through the streets by the strongest men, the women mourning their loss, their keening grief.

But for the best description of hubris Herodotus takes the biscuit and we're left with nemesis language ends, poetry dies with the poet's death

All artifice expelled with the final breath as carefully chosen words are no longer required apart from the eulogy, it is clear, despite your feel for rhythm, rhyme serves no purpose, the patterns of the spoken word, the eulogy demands that the patterns are set in four/four time.

It's in the text, it is, of course it is, the best critic will say, read the text, Thucydides for war. Back in Metepec, above the volcano, in a clear blue sky, a distant plane practices manoeuvres, the roar of its jets a back-ground noise emphasizing the peace we desire. And for peace, a settled way, justice, there's always Plato, no text, context, pretext, subtext ever better prepared.

Read the text of the poem, consider, the enjambments. Over time they will help focus on the next line and then the next, until it is over, you sit holding a finger between the pages, to mark your place, re-reading the Greeks, who advise be at peace with yourself your life lived in a seamless sea of time, rising, falling, ebbing, flowing, only stepping stones across a tidal flow of history, from birth to death.

That's poetry, she smiled, just words crafted out of the air and wind, just a notebook, a pencil, catching the words from the winds breath which blows unceasing across the waters, ebbing and flowing, rising, resisting. Here the tidal spray, lapping the hard stones on the gritty sand, the detritus of civilizations, empires and the store cup-board of history.

Declensions, the steady pendulum of this breathing earth, as tides rise and fall, speaks so eloquently of birth and death, islanding this boat shaped rock cluster as giants stepping stones across the tidal flow. Leading from what precedes to what may ever follow.

He finished his food and rose to leave. I'm sorry he said but it can't be helped. I will continue to write, to travel and eventually I will find the coffin, the one in which I will lie, as the mourners sing their elegies, before they lower me into this Mexican soil for my final, eternal rest.

Stay a while longer, she smiled through the smoke of another cigarette, more coffee? He shook his head gently. He rose to leave. Will I, she asked, see you again? He shook his head once more. There is more to this than just poetry he said, there is fiction, travel, there is crime reporting, God knows we have enough of that! There is a need for honesty, for realism, for visceral truth told bluntly. She studied the menu, I may, she said, stay for lunch. It was only then that the image came back to him of the dogs on the road. The sound of the bus as it hit them one by one, their howls, the snapping of breaking bones, their blood on the tarmac. He staggered and held on to the table. She looked up suddenly concerned, only to see him fading from view, disappearing into the dark shadows of the café, the shock on the waiters face transparent.

His death in an automobile accident was reported later that week. It had happened, en-route to Puebla, when the Mexico City express bus ran into a pack of wild dogs and careered off the road, hitting a concrete culvert and turning over three times before coming to rest in the gravel by the side of the highway.

Herodotus, after hubris, nemesis.

Lightning Source UK Ltd.
Milton Keynes UK
07 September 2010

159548UK00002B/73/P

9 781453 514160